Lullabies for End Times

Lullabies for End Times

poems by
Jennifer Bradpiece

~ 2020 ~

Lullabies for End Times
© Copyright 2020 Jennifer Bradpiece
All rights reserved. No part of this book may be used or reproduced in any manner whatsoever without written permission from either the author or the publisher, except in the case of credited epigraphs or brief quotations embedded in articles or reviews.

Editor-in-chief
Eric Morago

Associate Editors
Robin Fiorito & Victoria Lynne McCoy

Editor Emeritus
Michael Miller

Marketing Director
Dania Alkhouli

Marketing Assistant
Ellen Webre

Proofreader
José Enrique Medina

Front cover art
Giuliana Maresca

Back cover art
David Tripp

Author photo
Alexis Rhone Fancher

Book design
Michael Wada

Moon Tide logo design
Abraham Gomez

Lullabies for End Times
is published by Moon Tide Press

Moon Tide Press
6709 Washington Ave. #9297, Whittier, CA 90608
www.moontidepress.com

FIRST EDITION

Printed in the United States of America

ISBN # 978-1-7339493-9-2

In memory of Mom and Dad

Contents

Lullaby for Miss America	9
Lullaby for Afternoon	10
Lullaby for a Dog	11
Lullaby for Snooze Bars	13
Lullaby for My Niece	14
Lullaby for My Nephew	15
Lullaby for Children	16
Lullaby for a Politician	17
Lullaby for an American Ex-Pat	18
Lullaby for Four Letters	20
Lullaby for Gravity	21
Lullaby for Easter	22
Lullaby for the Dead	23
Lullaby for My Mother	25
Lullaby for Girls Who Still Play With Dolls at Night	26
Lullaby for a Friend	27
Lullaby for What We're Left With	29
Lullaby for Ovaries	30
Lullaby for a Drag Queen in Her Dressing Room	31
Lullaby for the Enemy	32
Lullaby for Venice	34
Lullaby for Division	36
Lullaby for My Lungs	37
Lullaby for the Moon	39
Lullaby for Thirsty Lawn Furniture	40
Lullaby for a Species	41
About the Author	*43*
Acknowledgments	*44*

We survive until, by sheer stamina, we escape into the dim innocence of our own adulthood and its forgetfulness.

–Katherine Dunn, *Geek Love*

Lullaby for Emergencies

A siren splits the night
like a diver unfolds through water
in a still pond.

Like no siren ever divided silence before.
Like the drink in my hand tickles my throat,
and scatters my thoughts like a shooter marble.

Below me, little things grow
between concrete slabs
despite everything.

Sad potted plants dangle off
loft windowsills.
Some reach a vine upwards
in vain. Others shrug in despair.

From somewhere up above me,
the siren cries out:
one sharp glowing ring-shaped punch
to the straight slate line of night sky.

Lullaby for Miss America

There she is
wrapped in red like waxed cheese.

She has been sculpted and sanded by
the balding god-head of moguls.
Someone else's sex patented
and stamped with approval, but wait…
The doll has shifted in her packaging,
has wandered out after dark as if she were anatomically correct,
has stabbed at subversion,
only transgressing the god who packaged her,
a brand name pasteurized.

In the end,
they will not disown her.
They will strip her down to her baby-white flesh
and fasten her up to their own glossy page.
A little Mary, reclaimed by commerce,
by the men who open and shut the Earth with their eyes.

Lullaby for Afternoon

Day pulls away, shadow-arms stretching toward light.
Dusk, a shadow-mime mocking meager accomplishments,
points sunlit shards onto piles of unopened books,
steak-stained pans, the leftover drippings of congealed ambition,
stiff like the clock's face in its five-past-four sneer.
Day collapses onto the couch, eases into the corner cushions
like an old dog desperate in its final hours,
haunches kicking, fetid tongue licking at its gut
as the room darkens in around its eyes.

Lullaby for a Dog

I will revisit a place
I wanted to stay.
I will take you with me.

I sink into the cloth hammock:
the cloudless sky, the Moroccan lantern
above my head
and the wooden slats breaking the sun's light
are all impossibly blue.

The Formica table is cold as January—
your ears are late July.

The hammock sways above your head
like a half-moon on a rocker.

You turn your dewy nose up
to nuzzle me, before a furtive flicker
of motion steals your eye:

A quail bobs its plumed head
as it parades down the soft dirt pathway.
You are captured by the staccato
motion of the bird until the sun warms
your back and tumbles you onto your side.
You stretch out, front paws reaching
over shaded cement.

You hear voices murmur.
There is the clamor of metal.

The long sprig of foxtail leaves
bends down just low enough for
you to take between your teeth.
As you chew the earthen taste of oat
hay seeps like tea onto your tongue,
such a different flavor from the sweet
and coppery green grass near your tail.

As your eyes begin to close
the Joshua Trees tease you
running wide figure eights in the breeze.
They look as your plush toys might
if they came to life and ran panicked,
puffy limbs waving, blind from the time
you chewed out their eyes.

The afternoon folds into dusk so slowly
each distinctive color and turn of shadow and light
is visible as individual beads on a child's abacus.

*A faint, awful sucking sound. A vial
is filled, then another.*

But come back with me
to the warm pavement below.
Well, cooling now.
Now the moon and sun face off
gently, and the sky goes indigo.

The silence here is so dense, listening
is like biting into rawhide. Over my head,
suddenly two sparrows...

Lullaby for Snooze Bars

One thousand things passed under my window,
all of them deadly.

The parade of corpses,
every one of them without feet.
I was grateful they passed almost in silence.

There was a carousel of centaurs:
part man, part machine.
I thought I recognized the faces,
but they passed me blindly, every one.

Ice skaters slid by like radio waves
with featureless faces and nonsense mouths.
I tried to echo them, but my lips couldn't form the words.

Dogs with metal tongues growled on the street,
swallowing mailboxes whole.
Delivery men chased them
with remote controls screaming, "Malfunction!"

There was text transposed in the air.
I had to read the lines vertically,
upset because I couldn't lie down.

White coats with huge eyes and no ears
climbed through my window,
renamed my organs and rearranged my bones.
I found my fingers attached to my neck,
had to write in a blind backbend.

My snooze bar became
a delete button.
I pressed it, and everything
reappeared.

Lullaby for My Niece

Handle the heirlooms with care.

Yes, the gilded cravings,
addiction poised hungers,
crystalline cut bowls on the highest
shelves faceted with neurosis,
all the hedonistic homes
that rent us out.

But don't be too shy to share

a heart, wide as a canyon,
words that try to leap the gap
or some magic paint brush,
instrument, song—

some lens to filter
our compromised world through.

If the pain should pass down,
unwelcome inheritance of flesh,
hold my hand.

If you find your hands deftly
mending with needle and thread
your own sweet limbs resurrected
in some sacred gothic graveyard,
take the end from the color red,
roll the spool backwards,
leave some trail for us to follow.

Lullaby for My Nephew

When you came along,
I no longer recognized myself.

You rearranged all of our faces:
dreams, desires, fears, strung on
yet severed at the cord.

The monsters aren't in your closet
or under your bed.
But don't turn on the TV, stand
too close to the microwave, ever get
your lover's name tattooed across your chest.

You were born bearing gifts:

a calm that could tame a tsunami,
a laugh that tickles the sun,
an ageless aura of Zen.

When your eyes light, a fairy smiles,
a gnome plays the grass flute,
a lion settles in a glen.

We will disappoint you. Forgive us.

If we are each born into this world
owing some debt, know
that you have already paid
with interest.

Lullaby for Children

I envy them too much
to have one.

Their infinite mouths,
mad things
uttering syllables detached
from discernible meaning.

The unprovoked screams
in crowded restaurants.

The inconsolable moan
at improbable altitudes in planes.

The things they do with food
when tiny green peas inspire
performance art instead of appetite.

I am still confused by the electric
fuse of life
pulsing through my own veins.
Too confounded to expand the cord
of my flesh into the blood and breath of another.

I rearrange the clutter inside
my own crowded room,
alphabetize my insomnia, press
my compulsions neatly on the floral slab,
needlepoint my neurosis into cushions.

In this asylum, only room for one.

Lullaby for a Politician

for dad

When I say, "I *knew* this would happen,"
my mother looks like she wants to slap me.

Who could blame her?

I'm portending my father
landing in the emergency room,
the very day the old dog passed,
with the same certainty one might lament
a full glass toppling off a table's edge.

Where were my minders?
I had nearly misplaced an entire continent.

I turn on the television to keep the younger dog company.

Ernest Cossart's Irish brogue gently chastises,
"Ah, there's a real piece of idiocy—woman's instinct—
every slab-sided female in the world is a crystal gazer—
she's magic. She can foretell the future—like a politician."

Flustered, I grab my water bottle, recheck the emergency number.

As I wheel around before closing the door,
I see Ginger Rogers, black and white in soft focus.
She spins around at her door, facing me
and an off-camera Cossart.

All the way down the hall her plucky voice follows me,
"And don't you worry about me, Pop,
'cause I can take care of myself alright!"

Lullaby for an American Ex-Pat

To be read with Marlene Dietrich's "Want to Buy Some Illusions" playing softly in the background...

The city is a woman.
Her eyes are Absinthe.
Her voice is ice.
When she speaks,
smoke pours from her nostrils
and floats up toward the diffusion
of starlight.

Her name could be Ashill,
or Siena, or Lyon.
But she is not merely quaint,
historic or scenic.
She is Praha. Timeless and ravaged,
dripping with garnets.

Her cobblestone legs open.

Here your losses are
crumbling stone steps
you navigate slowly.

You catch your reflection in the water
as you stroll past the Vltava.

You see scaffolding, think "skeleton."
The word "excavate" seems like flesh
you might penetrate. These words
become more intimate than
"hearth" or "home."

You love her because you find her less foreign
than your room back home, saturated
by the scent of musty words and turpentine.

She is a canvas,
a blank gessoed stare you recognize
in relief at her skyline.

You toast her with Becherovka, soda water,
and lime, watching jazz cabaret
alone at U Maleho Glena.
The black and white image
on the matchbooks reminds you
of Dietrich.

December brings less devoted tourists.
They flirt with her at the Christmas fair
in Old Town Square, sip her hot mulled wine
from paper cups, but you forgive her anything.

A new year marks the anniversary
of when she took you in, a refugee
of loss with a need to lose yourself
in something other.

You sit down at a café near the
Mala Strana: sketch a man with a thick
beard who sits alone in a corner,
a couple whispering into each other's ears,
a girl with sad eyes who keeps
resting her head on the heel of her hand.

You place the mug back on the saucer,
pick up your book and read afternoon straight
into evening. Years later you will swear
it was a book of poems by Lawrence,
but it may have been Rilke or Gilbert or a story by Kafka.
You tip an undetermined amount of Koruna,
nod at the waiter, slide a packet of sugar
between the pages to hold your place
and walk out into the night.

Behind your back, the city raises
one ironic eyebrow,
winks, and turns away.

Lullaby for Four Letters

there is no iconography too primitive
to house your exalted harp-strung syllables—oh,
when the moment disillusions sad eyes, I see you,
spectral over an enigmatic strip of bacon
at a table set for one. there in sweet need you settle
like an obvious epiphany pressing your name on my lips.
I need no sheets to conjure the other side, as I
am often guided to you by an unseen wall.
even with no hand on my skin, the soft hairs porcupine,
and I am a child mindfully kneeling before
the unspeakable unknown.

it's how you straddle my pillow like a preposition,
rattle the windowpanes, causing the space between
to bioluminescence. the saints snore until you enter,
those narcoleptic whores who require hair-shirts
to awaken from their ritualized transcription
of all our repentant mumblings.

altars can be found anywhere or counted like beads on fingers.
floating after sad nouns left behind, inhabiting no corporeal space,
you are perpetual motion, a dreamt gerund
tumbling innocent as a dervish or a prophet's puppy.
but mostly, penetrating entity, it is how you teach me
to come over and over and over again so almost
lovingly to the divine, despite all the Earth's profanity.

Lullaby for Gravity

The day penetrates, painfully blunt without you.
Cells protest, the awful choking head
is dragged from dreams to dawn,
bubbling toward awareness,
that gasping transition.
Always the desire to be unhooked,
wanting nothing of the light,
crisp air, possibilities of sky.
The line of consciousness tightens:
ties me not to the day's dock
but to a dinghy, that hardly holds the weight
of where you used to be.

Lullaby for Easter

Fruit ripens succulent on vines.
Sap warms sticky beneath tree bark.
Seeds spread roots into moist soil,
fragile shoots divide.
Buds bloom into bowls of nectar for bees
perpetuating fertility's frenzy.
Birds' abundant song disrupts
the last barren crispness of winter air.
Evening's eyes open to extra hours of light.

But the Latinate chorus sings only of death.
One man's death.
Resurrection, a warning:
the rebirth of only man's sins.

There are eggs,
no uterus, no womb.
Only one song, one death,
one million sins.

Lullaby for the Dead

with a line by Donald Justice

The dead don't
get around much anymore.
Doorstop coffins,
button eyes,
no chores—
maybe some easy gardening.
Useful in their rigor mortis
repose, maybe mannequins,
if you can stand the smell.
Taxidermy scarecrows,
androgynous monotone
dreams.
If you listen silently for
seven months you may
begin to decipher the didactic
sermons that sent them off.
Each popped like a pea out the sheath
of their leaf on the family tree.
Even postmortem
they grow and they grow
in the years populated
by the blood they left
or the skin they touched.
Bloated like drowning
victims, regardless of
how last breaths
were spent,
until they cannot hold the
soaked weight of their own
memory any longer.
Then like a vacant overgrown
lot, they deflate—
once again flat and vegetative—
uncoiled DNA.
Still, holidays are
less stressful

for the dead.
Their daybooks linger
open in the middle of
an empty table:
to-do lists short
as winter days
and no use for
day coats.

Lullaby for My Mother

My love was priest to my dying mother.
When he said: *Grace and compassion.*
When she confessed to finally courting silence.
When she said: *Sleep.*
When the television was blank and quiet.
When the lights were gratefully dimmed.
When the tree rats stampeded outside on the deck,
our vessel—sinking, sinking.
When we entered a celibate haze
of anesthetic "remember."
When he said: *You are brave.*
When one thousand cigarette butts
corked the gaps.
When the dog curled up on the sofa and sighed.
When she said: *Help me...*
When we barely coaxed the last blue
morphine communion down her dry throat.
When she said: *No more pain.*
When it rippled her softly back through time's keyhole.
When he said: *Jane, we are grateful.*
When the dog gingerly sniffed the bed,
bowed his head, and backed away.

Lullaby for Girls Who Still Play With Dolls at Night

Fee-fi-fo-fum—
Now I'm borrowed.
Now I'm numb.

—Anne Sexton, *The Addict*

set sail on oblong serrated apricot Alprazolam ships
in a pale blue Diazepam sky
from one Carisoprodol cloud to the next
marionette limbs bend in an Oxycodone
hoedown (that vicious Vicodin circle)
an opiate opera appreciated from barbiturate balconies
listening to Etodolac etudes
bring on Naltrexone neurosis
plant forensic flags on Amitriptyline acquisitions
(no more ambidextrous Amphetamine acrobatics)
instead Gabapentin gathers nerves gently
melts them down towards dreaming

Lullaby for a Friend

for HAW

Inside every patient there's a poet trying to get out...It seems to me that every seriously ill person needs to develop a style for his illness.

—Anatole Broyard

I am grateful
for the vision of you—
silk crepe monochrome dress flowing,
a sharp red beret on your head:
black and white meeting technicolor,
a study of contrasts, always always,
so like a woman I loved in the past.
Grateful for the poetry and the whiskey,
for the freight elevator that emptied our high octane
bodies into the onyx downtown streets.
You and I, suddenly, arms linked, weaving back and forth—
giddy plumes of cigarette smoke—
evaporating into our own oblivions.
Grateful for the art and word play afternoons,
which emptied us—new friends—into a vast piazza of *Déjà vu*.
Grateful for understanding
that dying the night
before April Fools' is so "you."
Grateful I was under stars
in your favorite desert
draining Mescal right from the bottle—
a toast you would approve.
Grateful for your gaze, distilling each thing
to its essence: your art in our world.
You tapped a PICC line into irony's vein,
bled it out on giant canvases and intricate collages.
Grateful for the puzzles that kept M sane.
Their pieces seemed to shrink and shrink,
like your hospice paintings, like you.
So often surrounded by soft muted colors,

those purple heather sheets,
yet punctuated by exotic bright:
your crimson crushed velvet caftan
your bright green Jelly flip-flops.
You were all the watercolors
and all the sharpies,
the tissue paper
and the scissors.
We grew up in the same town,
shared the same reference points:
both aliens there.
I didn't have to grow up next to you
to know you were born cool and impatient.
And born (like me) to pilot a boat
across the River Styx.
You knew the terrain
by heart:
cruel map
where familiarity stirs terror,
and every path is nearly
always another trap.

Lullaby for What We're Left With

Her last words
His last look
Last hospital visit
Clay paw prints
Worn gas mask
Rented death bed
Singed lace bra
Cobalt bobbed wig
Unsent birthday card
Stuffed trash bags
for Goodwill
Chipped nesting doll
Reverse mortgage
Adult diapers
Old photographs
of unknown faces
Blue morphine
Self-help books
Broken lava lamp
Private journal confession
Long probates
One thousand last cigarettes
and one very last December

Lullaby for Ovaries

The women are falling under sterile silver waves,
knives cutting out dangerous pearls.
Pearls carved by time cresting:
two decades, the wave falls
three decades under, four decades, five.

Women who cast words out on water,
paint on its oiled surface,
weave music from the air above sea,
adorn skins in shimmering scales of their own fashioning.
Women who create bodies of work rather than bodies within.

The doctors, those unimaginative navigators
of our vessels, ask "why?" and "when?"
Seeking to plant mermaids into gardens
like little Eves to seed
and split shoots that might save them,
yet anchor them into someone else's sands.

Now, I have harvested something foreign.
Been summoned to stand on
their diagnostic dock. They want me
unperfumed, stripped bare, my upper half turned,
breasts pressed between cold plastic,
two bookends
that might tell the end of the story between them.

Lullaby for a Drag Queen in Her Dressing Room

pungent perfume and musty sequins
only frame that stale cigarette smell
singeing feathers soft and curling
towards the plume's stiff spine
persona personified in glue
burning fake eyelashes flutter
(soft-bulb lights up, shutters drawn)
night burns like glitter up the nose
and her veins are on fire
again.

hothouse red hair
coils round that never still brow
arched or smeared down pancaked skin
diva today, dapper tomorrow
(they beat you in the alley
but scream for you on stage—
safest to hide in plain sight, they say)
so laugh off slights, line your rented smile
in deep ironic wine,
and work that broken hooker-heel-
foot-crammed-shin-splint-
wear-it-as-a-second-skin pain.
they'll come back for the obvious
lies. a rip and a tear in the old
social fabric: demand nothing,
question everything.

Lullaby for the Enemy

Don't you smell it—
musty between sleeves
of undusted books?
Tell me you feel it—
heavy, yet sharp
like a paper cut
buried in the stack
of unopened mail?
Can't you see it—sticking
out like a white sock
from the laundry
crumpled in the corner?
Listen—it's scraping through
the stereo
like matchsticks scratching themselves aflame.
There! In the hardwater-deposit
Rorschach blots. It's stuck in
used-toothpaste chalk
gnashed in the grout
between bathroom tiles.
It eats through my veins,
layers on my bones,
crystallizes between muscles,
tendons, joints, weighs my nerves
down until they mutiny, frenzied
and fried in the boat of my skin
on these sick waters. My brain cells
are cigarette burns in the old silk robe.
There is no trustworthy thread in this fabric
to loop over, re-stitch, or unwind.
I am undone. My sheets stretch
tightly over my open eyes.
Don't you see it? It's contaminating
the raw chicken sweating there on
the cutting board, dividing like cells
in a Petri dish?
Don't you know? The whole
goddamn world is toxic. I must put

it in order, control each hand-wielded
rationally dreamt thing. Look, look—
this is where it hides, how it finds me,
the way it comes—the pain—
it grows here, that enemy.

Lullaby for Venice

Remember the chimes,
the clock in the central square?
And we ran
over bridges arched like swans
through streets paved with merchants
bargaining for the time they keep
by counting foreign currency.
We stopped in barely lit shops
draped heavy with velvets
of crimson, green, and night-sky blue--
silk lined cloaks, feather hats,
lace trimmed masquerade masks
with ribbons to tie what's forgotten away.
Remember the chapel
that emptied into the ghetto like guilt?
The buildings full of hungry years,
still grumbling inside resilient stone.
And we ate alongside the canal
where you asked the water how
—in this enchanted place—
it could smell decayed.
I said the waters were papal veins
that carry the sins
from the heart of a city
that pulses with pleasure.
That's why lovers here are holy—
they lie in the gondolas, mouths open,
kindest to waters that
never need strain.
In the glass-blowing factory,
we watched men whisper life into bubbling shapes
of cobalt, emerald, and gold-flushed red,
like your face after dancing at the German beer hall.
The men conjure goblets, bottles, and
delicate beads—
like the strand I clutched in the taxi boat
as it took us away.
The beads that remembered the next day

in Florence, then Rome, then Pompeii,
where we bought cigarettes
from the Mafia,
giving money to the *capo*,
delaying a tour through the ancient city.
Remember when the Don rolled by,
his long Mercedes black and liquid,
how his men ran frenzied
like marbles scattered by a shooter?
That night on the ship bound for Greece
our luck changed at the casino bar
and we hardly had to pay.
And the mad woman
who shared her vodka,
gathered us close like a suspicious mother—
deep in our dark corner
so the ship attendants wouldn't see.
We nursed her bottle
to stories she told
of her youth in Brussels,
of the beauty she left there.
Her voice crackled like fire
on a crone's skin.
Her words came drifting, narrow fingers,
bands of purple cigarette smoke.
And she liked us because we were young
and our veins were lovely.
We took what little night she left us,
stumbling upstairs to your room,
and when we pulled down the bed,
there was none—
no room except for the sea.
We dissolved into the waves—
I was your Venus underwater.

Lullaby for Division

Unwelcome yellow light illuminates
crumpled dirty denim jeans
black lace bra, 36 C-cupping the air.
Somehow my heeled boots have claimed
ownership of your coiled socks.
Your corduroys entwine my halter top
echoing your honey, my ivory limbs.
Darkness practices addition.

Through open lids of windowsill
and subtly raised blinds,
beams filter, harass eyelids to flutter.
The crescent curve of our hips
resists the sun's circle outside.

The alarm clock rearranges
the silence, our dreams, our bodies.
Sunlight subtracts.

Your chest hairs tickle my back
as the singular cell of our warmth divides.

Lullaby for My Lungs

The tuner bird now nests,
now thrums,
in its cage of bone.
Plays harp of cat gut strings
by the red light
that dictates my resonant streams.
Sisyphean translator
at the first breath's strum.
That sought to home
that homed to seek
from its first beat—
under the weight of words
and through that escape room of language
that forever unhomes.
Breath that strained to decipher
until it found translation in plumes
clearer than consonants.
That let me site my body there.
That allowed me into yours
the way that clouds might
straddle continents between oceans,
sip moon tides and stir the storms to tea.
That we might sip, and we sipped
and we shared above the undertow
beneath its wingspan.
And now the bird is full and fat
and red-breasted, bursting—
full of its own song—
soon the only hymn I'll have to share,
between the bars of bone,
each porous easement;
the only pitch audible.
And the view from here is red
and veined and pulsing—quickened
by every foam-crested wave.
Each boat of my lungs shudders
when I am still—
the vast waters shimmer, shifting

just as they always did.
Now, a symphony of memory glows
wild, drowns me out, fastens me
to each red pulsing light.
I am wrapped in echo and echo,
can see with clarity, and must
hold the bird that sings to me
with gentle hands.
I whisper back soft benediction,
place to its beak a megaphone
projecting past where I could never
have gone, or stayed without
growing song.

Lullaby for the Moon

Full, it is Him—
a bold portrait
staring straight ahead

or a Picasso sliced
jack-o-lantern
wise yet comically
cratered in turns.

The crescent
is all Her,
waxing or waning,

a porcelain breast
slipped loose
from black satin.

Lullaby for Thirsty Lawn Furniture

the chairs hunker down
under layers of misuse
and dust. the air shimmies.

the cracking cushions know
those vast consumptive stars
better than any single eye
combined with any other.

inside, the acid porcupine quills
drip, sting velvet nerve endings,
those tiny pink pins quivering
at the edge of agreeable dissonance.

outside the unkempt layers melt,
skin sliding off the bone
white moon, the black sky
two charcoaled lungs of night.

the music goes straight
through, a marrow song
beating a silk drum muffled
in a string tendon quartet.

something of the moon is borrowed;
an extrapolation of stars,
the missing note a key
transposed on skin.

the rain on the roof
is a tin drum, a brass band,
a whole bone symphony.

Lullaby for a Species

The humans had a strange run.
They always thought
they were talking to each other.

They licked their fingers to paper
and folded up their hearts,
but stuffed them into sock drawers.

Paper cut deeper
than daggers
until the keyboard—

the tap-tap of resonant notes,
of dissonant notes.
They used them to strike,

but could not hear the music.
They signed their souls to Truth,
but seldom knew honesty.

Desperate to be heard,
they forgot
how to listen.

Now every window
lights an author,
audience dissolving.

Obsessed with finding
themselves,
each hallway grew mirrors.

All they desired
was there in the reflection
of the Other.

As ages passed, they created
experts for finding what they lost,
but forgot how to see.

Sometimes, though,
they saw each other just
before leaving.

About the Author

Jennifer Bradpiece was born and raised in the multifaceted muse, Los Angeles, where she still resides. She loves to collaborate with multi-media artists on projects. Her poetry has been nominated for a Pushcart Prize and published in various anthologies, journals, and online zines, including *Redactions*, *The Common Ground Review*, and *The Bacopa Literary Review*.

Acknowledgments

My sincere gratitude to the following journals where these poems have been previously published, or are forthcoming:

Anti-Heroin Chic: "Lullaby for What We're Left With" (published as "What we're Left with Sometimes")

The Bicycle Review: "Lullaby for Girls who Still Play with Dolls at Night"

The Chickasaw Plum: "Lullaby for Gravity" (as "Gravity")

The Collidescope: "Lullaby for Thirsty Lawn Furniture" and "Lullaby for Four Letters" (as "Ode to Four Letters")

Degenerate Literature: "Lullaby for a Drag Queen"

The Examiner.com: "Lullaby for Miss America" (as "Miss America")

On Loss Anthology: "Lullaby for a Dog" and "Lullaby for the Dead" (as "Daybook of the Dead")

January Review: "Lullaby for an American Ex-Pat"

Mad Poets Review: "Lullaby for Children" (as "Children")

Moria: "Lullaby for Emergencies" and "Lullaby for my Mother"

Panoply, A Literary Zine: "Lullaby for a Politician"

Poetic Diversity: "Lullaby for Division" (as "Re-arranging the Night")

A Poet is a Poet no Matter How Tall Anthology: "Lullaby for my Niece" and "Lullaby for my Nephew"

Requiem Magazine: "Lullaby for Snooze Bars" (as "Techno-Dreams")

Short Poems Ain't got Nobody to Love Anthology: "Lullaby for Afternoon" (as "Afternoon")

"Miss America" was nominated for the Sundress Award (Best of the Web Nominee) 2014

Vast Gratitude

To my sine qua non, Boris; my partner in all things. Thank you for allowing me to turn you into a co-editor. Our process always helps me to find the direction I need to go and organize my head of bees.

Thank you to my crazy-talented Bad Ass Boob Poets who I'm so grateful to work with and know. And, specifically, Chrys Tobey—you talented power-house and beautiful friend—without you I wouldn't have been able to, so many times...

My cosmic space-sister, Giuliana Maresca—endless gratitude for your strange-creature-kinship and your art. I love sharing worlds and trading visions.

Love and thanks to my blood and found families. Thank you for always doing your best to see me and love me.

Big thank you to Eric Morago and Moon Tide Press for your kindness and patient guidance in landing this little ship.

In everything I write is the influence and guidance of every mentor I've ever had. Without finding them, I would have been lost or stuck many times over. Special thanks to WW, GA, & BC. Writing is a more communal process than many think.

Which leads me to express gratitude for our diverse and brilliant L.A. poetry scene. I appear and disappear depending on my health. The folx I've been inspired by here surprise me when I peek back out from my lair by remembering me and by always showing me generosity and kindness when we cross paths.

Patrons

Moon Tide Press would like to thank the following people for their support in helping publish the finest poetry from the Southern California region. To sign up as a patron, visit www.moontidepress.com or send an email to publisher@moontidepress.com.

Anonymous
Robin Axworthy
Conner Brenner
Bill Cushing
Susan Davis
Peggy Dobreer
Dennis Gowans
Alexis Rhone Fancher
Hanalena Fennel
Half Off Books & Brad T. Cox
Jim & Vicky Hoggatt
Michael Kramer
Ron Koertge & Bianca Richards
Ray & Christi Lacoste
Zachary & Tammy Locklin
Lincoln McElwee
David McIntire
José Enrique Medina
Andrew November
Michael Miller & Rachanee Srisavasdi
Michelle & Robert Miller
Terri Niccum
Ronny & Richard Morago
Jennifer Smith
Andrew Turner
Rex Wilder
Mariano Zaro

Also Available from Moon Tide Press

Crabgrass World, Robin Axworthy (2020)
Contortionist Tongue, Dania Ayah Alkhouli (2020)
The only thing that makes sense is to grow, Scott Ferry (2020)
Dead Letter Box, Terri Niccum (2019)
Tea and Subtitles: Selected Poems 1999-2019, Michael Miller (2019)
At the Table of the Unknown, Alexandra Umlas (2019)
The Book of Rabbits, Vince Trimboli (2019)
Everything I Write Is a Love Song to the World, David McIntire (2019)
Letters to the Leader, HanaLena Fennel (2019)
Darwin's Garden, Lee Rossi (2019)
Dark Ink: A Poetry Anthology Inspired by Horror (2018)
Drop and Dazzle, Peggy Dobreer (2018)
Junkie Wife, Alexis Rhone Fancher (2018)
The Moon, My Lover, My Mother, & the Dog, Daniel McGinn (2018)
Lullaby of Teeth: An Anthology of Southern California Poetry (2017)
Angels in Seven, Michael Miller (2016)
A Likely Story, Robbi Nester (2014)
Embers on the Stairs, Ruth Bavetta (2014)
The Green of Sunset, John Brantingham (2013)
The Savagery of Bone, Timothy Matthew Perez (2013)
The Silence of Doorways, Sharon Venezio (2013)
Cosmos: An Anthology of Southern California Poetry (2012)
Straws and Shadows, Irena Praitis (2012)
In the Lake of Your Bones, Peggy Dobreer (2012)
I Was Building Up to Something, Susan Davis (2011)
Hopeless Cases, Michael Kramer (2011)
One World, Gail Newman (2011)
What We Ache For, Eric Morago (2010)
Now and Then, Lee Mallory (2009)
Pop Art: An Anthology of Southern California Poetry (2009)
In the Heaven of Never Before, Carine Topal (2008)
A Wild Region, Kate Buckley (2008)
Carving in Bone: An Anthology of Orange County Poetry (2007)
Kindness from a Dark God, Ben Trigg (2007)
A Thin Strand of Lights, Ricki Mandeville (2006)
Sleepyhead Assassins, Mindy Nettifee (2006)
Tide Pools: An Anthology of Orange County Poetry (2006)
Lost American Nights: Lyrics & Poems, Michael Ubaldini (2006)

www.ingramcontent.com/pod-product-compliance
Lightning Source LLC
Chambersburg PA
CBHW031218090426
42736CB00009B/971